LADY LEGENDS ALPHABET

Words by Robin Feiner

A is for **A**melia Earhart. This aviation pioneer, the first woman to fly solo across the Atlantic, continues to inspire generations of women to reach for the sky.

B is for Beyoncé.
Believing in herself from
an early age is what helped
'Queen Bey' become a star
and realize her destiny.

**C is for Marie Curie.
A Nobel Prize in Physics,
and another in Chemistry,
has enshrined her as one
of the most influential
scientists in history.**

D is for Princess **D**iana. The 'People's Princess' used her influence to make a real difference for those less fortunate.

E is for **E**llen DeGeneres. This comedian, actress and larger than life personality, put her career on the line by staying true to herself.

Ff

F is for **F**rida Kahlo. Her vibrant and honest self-portraits have seen this Mexican artist become an icon for feminists everywhere.

G is for Indira Gandhi. As the only female Prime Minister of India, she powerfully stood up for the rights of women, earning her the title, 'Woman of the Millennium.'

I is for Iris Apfel.
This celebrated fashion icon hasn't let old age stand in her way, becoming more zany, flamboyant and famous with each year.

Jj

J is for Jane Austen. Back when a lady was expected to be proper, she wrote about strong, independent women.

Kk

K is for Helen Keller. Unable to see or hear, she overcame her disabilities and taught the world not to underestimate the deaf and the blind.

L is for Annie Leibovitz. A photographer whose intimate portraits defined the image of so many iconic celebrities.

Mm

M is for **M**aya Angelou. This highly revered American poet, singer, memoirist, and civil rights activist, was a bold spokesperson for African-Americans and women.

Nn

N is for Florence **N**ightingale. 'The Lady with the Lamp' fought tirelessly for women's rights in Britain and taught nurses the power of compassion.

O is for **O**prah Winfrey. With the talent to connect, she's gone on to become a television personality with incredible popularity and influence, inspiring women from all backgrounds.

Oo

Pp

P is for Rosa Parks.
When told to give up her
seat on the bus for a white
person, she bravely stood
her ground and ignited
America's Civil Rights
Movement.

Q is for **Q**ueen Cleopatra. Her charm, intelligence and devotion to her people, made her a popular ruler and role model for women.

R is for J. K. **R**owling. With the dream of becoming a writer, she put her all behind one magic idea that transformed her from rags to riches.

S is for Meryl **S**treep. Some call her the 'greatest actress of her generation,' others think of her as the 'greatest actor of all time.'

T is for Mother **T**eresa. She moved to India and dedicated her life to helping the poor and the sick. For giving as she did, the church declared her a saint.

U is for Galina **Ulanova.** One of the greatest ballet dancers of all time, she captivated audiences with her every move and raised ballet into a popular art form.

V is for **V**ivienne Westwood. As a famous punk fashion designer, she uses her influence to campaign for human rights and the environment.

Ww

W is for Serena and Venus **W**illiams. After beating every competitor and record on the tennis court, these sisters have taken on racism and sexism as well.

X is for **X**ena Warrior Princess. Fighting hard for the greater good, Xena has earned a special place in the hearts and minds of feminists.

Y is for Malala **Y**ousafzai. From a very early age she has campaigned fearlessly for the education of underprivileged women, earning her the Nobel Peace Prize.

Z is for **Z**aha Hadid.
The buildings she designed
rewrote the rule book,
earning her the title
'Queen of the Curve' and
big awards previously
reserved for men.

LADY LEGENDS ALPHABET
www.alphabetlegends.com

Published by Alphabet Legends Pty Ltd in 2018
Created by Beck Feiner
Copyright © Alphabet Legends Pty Ltd 2018

UNICEF AUSTRALIA
A portion of the Net Proceeds from the sale of this book
are donated to UNICEF.

978-0-6482616-0-5

Printed in Canada

**EXPLORE THESE LEGENDARY ALPHABETS
& MORE AT WWW.ALPHABETLEGENDS.COM**